COMPETENCY SKILLS—MATHEMATICS
By Anne Leschen & Judy Tisdale

Table of Contents

Teacher's Guide

Page 1: Math Review
This page contains review problems for students to work. Correct this page with the class so students may ask questions about difficult problems. Students may give themselves a score on the page if they desire. It is suggested that students keep the following pages in a folder or a binder. This is the first page of their book.

Page 2: Reading Recipes
This page uses recipes as the basis for a review of basic number operations. The measuring cups illustrated are standard measures. Be sure to point out that if using a metric conversion chart, a cup will equal 236 milliliters, not 250 milliliters as illustrated on measuring cups.

Page 3: Understanding Banking
Simple banking procedures are explained on this page. A sample check, check stub, and deposit slip are shown. Addition and subtraction are used in computing problems related to banking.

Page 4: Spending Money
On this page students will use a menu to review math operations. It is important that they read the menu and the problems carefully. Students will learn that they may possibly save money if they read carefully.

Page 5: Spending Money
This page is an exercise in reading directions as well as a math review. A sample order form from a catalog is used as the basis for practicing number operations. As on page 4, students will learn that careful reading can be practical.

Page 6: Reading a Schedule
A sample student schedule is pictured at the top of this page. Students will figure time as well as proportion. Additional practice can be given by asking students to figure time with their own schedules.

Page 7: Studying Graphs
A circle graph and a bar graph are used to teach graph skills. To reinforce this review, the class might graph time spent on their chores at home, their own allowance, or something they could convert to fractions for use on a circle graph.

Page 8: Sports Math
This page covers two types of math used in sports. The first example teaches students how to figure a team's percentage while the second exercise teaches averages. Some students may be able to share other ways that math is used in sports. As an additional assignment, have the class bring team standings from a newspaper to school and have them compute the percentages or averages.

Page 9: Computing Sales Tax
Point out to the class that states have different tax rates. Have students find out what the tax rate is where they live and give them sample problems to compute.

Page 10: Consumer Discounts
Problems are given using percentage-off discounts. Students will read the advertisement at the top of the page and compute the discounts using varying percentage rates. Careful reading of the advertisement is essential.

Page 11: Travel Trivia
This page covers two areas of travel, reading a map with a scale and figuring gasoline miles per gallon. A sample map is pictured. Students will also figure the cost of filling the pictured cars with gasoline. It would be helpful to discuss why MPG is now an important consumer term.

Page 12: Review Test
This test covers information given in the first part of this book. It is a review of math operations and a practical application of the material covered. It may or may not be given as a timed test.

Page 13: Using Fractions
This page uses product information as the basis for fraction review. Students will fill in a chart using simple math. Exercises also include reducing fractions to lowest terms.

Page 14: Geometry
Students will identify geometric shapes and review terms such as perpendicular, parallel, etc.

Page 15: Perimeter, Area, and Volume
The formulas for figuring perimeter, area, and volume are given. Additional practice may be given using familiar places for students to figure size, such as determining the area, perimeter, and even volume of the classroom or a room at home.

Page 16: Best Buys
Unit pricing is explained on this page. Students will use simple math to determine which product is the best buy.

Page 17: Earnings and Deductions
This page gives the students a detailed look at earnings and deductions. This page requires careful reading and computation. It would be helpful to the students to check this page together.

Page 18: Studying Charts
This page uses a weather report as a basis for reviewing percentages. Students must answer questions using percentages, interpreting a chart and comparing degrees Celsius and Fahrenheit.

Page 19: Working with Decimals
This page reviews decimals, percents, and adding and multiplying decimals.

Page 20: Review Test
This page is a review of the material covered in this book.

ANSWERS

Page 1

1,704	13,958	2,978	192,931	114,000
	202			

1,020,540	55,590	201,020	91 r 1	11906.10
3.354				

			2 1/2	14/39
231,176	$355.25	1	23/30	15/32
2,442	834,000	164.7	$62.57	26.64
100	$1.00	.0036	175	
250	1/4	25,000	7 lb. 13 oz.	
5 r 50	400	2500	75	

				621.17
119,979	5,504,595	166.67		72

			1/12	
31 1/2	31 r 7	1 1/16	0	
1 7/16	1 4/5	1/16	29/50	

Page 2

1. 1 cup flour, ½ t. baking powder,
   1 cup sugar, 1 cup oatmeal, 4 T. cream,
   4 T. corn syrup, 2 t. vanilla
2. 1½ cups flour, 1½ cups sugar, 3 t. vanilla
3. 6 oz.
4. 16 oz.
5. yes
6. 500 ml
7. 4
8. ½ t.
9. yes
10. ¼ cup
11. ½ cup
12. 250 ml
13. 1 1/3
14. 1 1/2
15. 375 ml

1 cup flour would require ½ cup salt.
8 cups flour would need 4 cups salt.
5 cups flour would require 2½ cups salt.
3 cups flour would need 1½ cups salt.

1. 11 cups   2. ½ cup   3. 1 to 2

Page 3

1. +, − 2. $10.00 3. $.80 4. yes, $186.50

1. 2   2. no   3. $172.00

1. $75.80   4. $38.75
2. $935.00   5. $186.65
3. $352.00

Page 4

1. less, $2.47   4. $5.87
2. $2.73   5. Answers will vary.
3. $1.35

Page 5

1. $3.00   5. yes, $26.99, $3.01
2. $23.97, $32.97 6. 1 belt and 1 shirt
3. $8.00, $10.00 $10.99
4. $18.99, $50.97 7. no

Page 6

1. 2 hrs., 2½ hrs., 1 hr. 45 min., 1 hr.
   3 hrs., 1½ hrs., 30 min.
2. yes, 1 hr., 10 min.

Page 6 Continued

3. 5 min.
4. no, no, yes
5. No, art is 35 min. - break is 15 min.
6. four days out of five
7. 60 minutes three days a week
8. 3 hours, 50 minutes a day
9. 2½ hours a week
10. 5 to 3
11. 2½ hours to 2 hours

Page 7

1. Lunch, $3.00, Boy Scouts, Stamps, $1.00
2. Yes, 0
3. $2.00, $1.00, 50¢
4. $4.50
1. 2000   4. January
2. 1000   5. 5000, greater
3. 3500

Page 8

1. .714 2. .500 3. .500 4. .429
5. 70 total games, .400 percentage
   133 total games, .827 percentage
   50 total games, .640 percentage
1. 164.5   2. 113.7   3. 78.1

Page 9

1. $9.82 + $.59 = $10.41
2. $6.06 + $.36 = $6.42
3. Pencils - $.48
   Erasers - $.48
   Blotters - $.25
   Glue - $.86
   Total - $3.18
4. $.20
1. .02   2. .04   3. .07   4. .05
1. $.04   4. $.50
2. $.49   5. $.10
3. $.32

Sales Tax	Total Cost
$.48	$12.48
$.15	$ 3.15
$.48	$ 8.48

Page 10

1.

Bathing Suit	Shoes	Scarf
$26.00	$17.00	$10.00
20%	33%	10%
$ 5.20	$ 5.61	$ 1.00
$20.80	$11.39	$ 9.00

Total $41.19
2. $62.50
3. $1.80, $9.00
4. 30¢, 45¢, 15%
5. $17.10, $15.39

Page 11

1. 6 miles   5. 3 miles
2. 1 mile longer 6. 7 miles
3. 1 inch, 2 miles 7. 6 inches
4. Cedar, Walnut, Pine, Elm

Page 11 Continued

A $18.70, 340 miles   C $16.50, 465 miles
B $24.20, 308 miles   D $19.80, 450 miles

Page 12

1. 65¢
2. $20.55
3. 39¢
4. $147.06
5. one hr. thirty min.
6. $351.80
7. 3/4 cup
8. 4 inches
9. .567
10. .702
11. 196.8
12. the $2.00 notebook
13. 1 1/3 cups
14. $25.30
15. 264 miles
16. 3 hrs. 30 min.

Page 13

	4 Servings	6 Servings
Water	1 1/3 cups	2 cups
Milk		1 cup
Butter	2 Tbsp.	
Salt		3/4 tsp.
Potato Flakes	2 cups	3 cups

1. See chart above.
2. 6 cups
3. twice as much
4. 4 cups
5. 2 cups, 2 2/3 cups
6. 1/3 5/6 4/5 3/4 3/4 1/3
   9/10 1/2 1/3 1/7 1/5 1/6

1. 3 T. drink mix + 16 oz. water = 2 servings
2. 4½ T.
3. 6 T.
4. 5/6

Page 14

1. rectangle
2. cylinder
3. cube
4. parallelogram
5. perpendicular
6. 90°
7. 180°
8. a 90° angle
9. ray
10. pentagon
11. It has 2 more 60° angles.
12. 360°
13. 360°
14. 6 sides
15. 8 sides
16. 4 sides
17. opposite sides parallel
18. form right angles
19. passes through the center of a circle
20. distance around circle

Page 15

1. 15 sq. units
2. 15 tiles
3. 16 units
4. 3 sq. units
5. 27 cu. units
6. C - 20 cubic units
   D - 16 cubic units
   E - 12 cubic units
7. 88 sq. ft., 22 sq. ft.
8. 32', 2'

Page 16

1 oz. = 8¢ or 1 oz. = 6¢
1. soup   6 for 90¢
   crackers 1 lb. $.47
   olives   10 oz. for $3.00

Page 16 Continued

2. $4.37

orange juice	$ .40	pizza crust	$1.54
towels	$1.20	pepperoni	$3.00
toothpaste	2	soda	$1.02
dog food	$ .32	chips	$1.00
pizza sauce	2	lettuce	$ .34

Page 17

1. yes
2. federal withholding tax
3. the amount the employee takes home
4. FICA
5. $37.20
6. the amount deducted or earned thur far this year
7. $6.00
8. 6

Page 18

1. Friday
2. 100%
3. June, 3½ in.
4. 4 inches
5. yes
6. July and August
7. 25 degrees
8. 100 degrees, 180 degrees
9. smaller
10. 5.4°

Page 19

1. 9
2. 5
3. 8923.755
4. 9923.765
5. 8923.8

1. 5.2
2. 18.35
3. 235.08
4. 605.03
5. 1525.5
6. 200.489

1. 125 9/1000
2. 76 7/10
3. 900 1/10
4. 5 5/10
5. 999 9/10
6. 1 2/10

1. 75%
2. 12 1/2%
3. 50%
4. 90%
5. 60%
6. 66 2/3%
7. 25%
8. 33 1/3%

1. 209.35
2. 35.441
3. 921.12
4. 16.11
5. 57.09
6. 79.87

1. 171.6 2. 269.64 3. 3.6 4. .0040

Page 20

1. 1 1/2
2. 432.54
3. 3 3/4
4. 437 feet
5. intersect at right angles
6. 1728 sq. in.
7. 5 lb. bag
8. 1¢ a lb.
9. $18.75
10. 61.7 degrees
11. 75 feet
12. 5/8
13. 1/4
14. $56.00
15. 1 1/10
16. Team A has won a higher percentage of games.

Competency Skills - Math

Math Review

Work the following problems carefully. Remember to keep columns straight and to write numbers legibly. When working with decimals, round to nearest hundredths.

$$\begin{array}{r} 241 \\ 669 \\ 582 \\ +\ 212 \\ \hline \end{array}$$

$1{,}779 + 3{,}113 + 9{,}066 =$ _____

$58 + 77 + 38 + 29 =$ _____

$$\begin{array}{r} 11{,}201 \\ -\ 8{,}223 \\ \hline \end{array}$$

$$\begin{array}{r} 801{,}474 \\ -\ 608{,}543 \\ \hline \end{array}$$

$$\begin{array}{r} 5700 \\ \times\ 20 \\ \hline \end{array}$$

$$\begin{array}{r} 110{,}333 \\ 784{,}707 \\ +\ 125{,}500 \\ \hline \end{array}$$

$$\begin{array}{r} 545 \\ \times\ 102 \\ \hline \end{array}$$

$$\begin{array}{r} 8740 \\ \times\ 23 \\ \hline \end{array}$$

$63\ \overline{)\ 5734}$ $.82\ \overline{)\ 9763}$

$$\begin{array}{r} 67.08 \\ \times\ .05 \\ \hline \end{array}$$

$$\begin{array}{r} 407 \\ \times\ 568 \\ \hline \end{array}$$

$$\begin{array}{r} \$7.89 \\ \$329.00 \\ +\ \$18.36 \\ \hline \end{array}$$

$$\begin{array}{r} \frac{5}{12} \\ +\ \frac{7}{12} \\ \hline \end{array}$$

$\frac{5}{8} \div \frac{1}{4} =$ _____

$\frac{23}{24} \times \frac{4}{5} =$ _____

$\frac{7}{13} \times \frac{2}{3} =$ _____

$\frac{5}{8} \times \frac{3}{4} =$ _____

$$\begin{array}{r} 111 \\ \times\ 22 \\ \hline \end{array}$$

$$\begin{array}{r} 1{,}775{,}000 \\ -\ 941{,}000 \\ \hline \end{array}$$

$$\begin{array}{r} 8235 \\ \times\ .02 \\ \hline \end{array}$$

$\$42.98 + \$17.90 + \$1.69 =$ _____

$$\begin{array}{r} 888 \\ \times\ .03 \\ \hline \end{array}$$

20% of $500 =$ _____

10% of $\$10.00 =$ _____

$$\begin{array}{r} .09 \\ \times\ .04 \\ \hline \end{array}$$

$\frac{1}{2}$ of $350 =$ _____

$\frac{1}{4}$ of $1000 =$ _____

$\frac{1}{2} \times \frac{1}{2} =$ _____

50% of $50{,}000 =$ _____

$$\begin{array}{r} 4 \text{ lb. } 5 \text{ oz.} \\ +\ 3 \text{ lb. } 8 \text{ oz.} \\ \hline \end{array}$$

$125\ \overline{)\ 675}$ $250\ \overline{)\ 100{,}000}$ $.50\ \overline{)\ 1250}$ 75% of $100 =$ _____

$1.39 + 450.03 + 169.75 =$ _____

$$\begin{array}{r} 120{,}004 \\ -\ 25 \\ \hline \end{array}$$

$$\begin{array}{r} 609{,}834 \\ 4{,}871{,}095 \\ +\ 23{,}666 \\ \hline \end{array}$$

$.45\ \overline{)\ 75.0}$

50% of $144 =$ _____

$\frac{1}{2} \times 63 =$ _____

$503 \div 16 =$ _____

$$\begin{array}{r} \frac{5}{16} \\ +\ \frac{3}{4} \\ \hline \end{array}$$

$\frac{5}{6} - \frac{3}{4} =$ _____

$\frac{9}{15} - \frac{3}{5} =$ _____

$\frac{7}{8} + \frac{1}{4} + \frac{5}{16} =$ _____

$\frac{9}{10} \div \frac{1}{2} =$ _____

$\frac{1}{2} \times \frac{1}{8} =$ _____

$\frac{2}{25} + \frac{1}{2} =$ _____

Reading Recipes

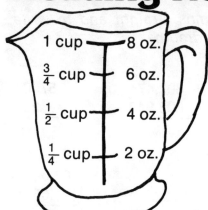

Oatmeal Lace Cookies

$\frac{1}{2}$ cup flour   2 T. cream

$\frac{1}{4}$ t. baking powder   2 T. light corn syrup

$\frac{1}{2}$ cup sugar   1 t. vanilla

$\frac{1}{2}$ cup oatmeal

Mix ingredients well.
Drop by $\frac{1}{4}$ t. on ungreased baking sheet.
Bake at 375 degrees.

Using the above recipe and the measuring cups pictured on this page, answer the following questions. Metric conversion charts will not give the same measurements of milliliters for one cup.

1. Give the amounts of each ingredient if the recipe was doubled. _____
_____

2. If the recipe was tripled, how much flour would be used? _____
    Sugar? _____   Vanilla? _____

3. How many ounces (oz.) in $\frac{3}{4}$ cup? _____

4. How many ounces in 2 cups? _____

5. Is 125 ml. the same as $\frac{1}{2}$ cup, using the measuring cup above? _____

6. How many milliliters in 2 cups? _____

7. How many $\frac{1}{4}$ teaspoons in one teaspoon? _____

8. If the recipe is doubled, how many teaspoons of baking powder are used? _____

9. Is the amount of cream used the same as the amount of corn syrup? _____

10. 2 oz. = _____cup

11. 125 ml. = _____ cup

12. 1 cup = _____ ml.

13. $\frac{2}{3} + \frac{2}{3}$ = _____

14. $\frac{3}{4} + \frac{3}{4}$ = _____

15. $1\frac{1}{2}$ cups = _____ ml.

A recipe for making dough for Christmas ornaments calls for 2 parts flour and one part salt to be mixed with enough water to make a stiff dough.
Which of the following statements would be true if the recipe was enlarged or decreased? Underline the true statements.

1 cup flour would require $\frac{1}{2}$ cup salt.   5 cups flour would require $2\frac{1}{2}$ cups salt.

4 cups flour would require 3 cups salt.   2 cups flour would need 4 cups salt.

2 cups flour would need 1 cup water.   3 cups flour would need $1\frac{1}{2}$ cups salt.

8 cups flour would need 4 cups salt.   5 cups flour would need $2\frac{1}{2}$ cups water.

1. How many cups of flour would you need if you used $5\frac{1}{2}$ cups salt? _____

2. How many cups of flour would you need if you used $\frac{1}{4}$ cup salt? _____

3. The ratio of salt to flour is: 1 to 2   2 to 1   1 to 4

2   Competency Skills—Math

Understanding Banking

Study this sample personal check and the attached check stub.

Check Stub	Check
NO. 556 DATE *Sept 19, 19 82* TO *Rudolph's Drug Store* FOR *Prescription* BALANCE *$684.43* DEPOSIT *$186.50* TOTAL *$870.93* AM'T THIS CHECK *$10.80* NEW BALANCE *$860.13*	*Sept. 19,* 19 *82* 556 PAY TO THE ORDER OF *Rudolph's Drug Store* $ *10.80* *Ten dollars and 80/100* DOLLARS NAME OF BANK *Signature* 12345678 006 500 123

A personal check may be written for cash, for the amount of purchase at a place of business, or to another person. A check stub is a record of money spent (subtracted) and money deposited (added) to the account.

Answer these questions about the check stub and check.

1. How many mathematical operations are used on a check stub? Fill in the circle before each operation that is used.

    ○ +   ○ —   ○ X   ○ ÷

2. What is the dollar amount of this check? _____
3. What is the cents amount? _____
4. Was a deposit made on this check stub? _____ How much? _____

A deposit slip is used each time money is added to a checking account.

NAME OF BANK	CASH	CURRENCY	
		COIN	
DATE *11-7* 19 *82*		CHECKS (list singly)	*$75 00*
			97 00
		Total From Other Side	*0*
006 500 123		NET DEPOSIT	*$172 00*

1. How many checks were deposited? _____   2. Was any currency deposited? _____
3. The total deposit should read: ○ $75.00   ○ $172.00   ○ $97.00

Work these banking problems.

1. Deposit $53.05 + $17.00 + $5.75 =
    ○ $75.08   ○ $75.80   ○ $78.50
2. Subtract $175.00 from a balance of $1,110.00.
    ○ $1935.00   ○ $955.00   ○ $935.00
3. Subtract $48.00 from a balance of $325.00 and then deposit $75.00.
    ○ $352.00   ○ $277.00   ○ $325.00
4. Subtract $23.50 and $62.75 from a balance of $125.00.
    ○ $86.25   ○ $38.75   ○ $80.75
5. Deposit $183.15 and $3.50. The total deposit is:
    ○ $180.06   ○ $176.65   ○ $186.65

Spending Money

When going to a restaurant, it is important to be able to read the menu and estimate the bill before ordering. This will keep you from overspending.

BURGER HUT MENU

SANDWICHES		SIDE ORDERS		DRINKS	
Burger Delight	$ .97	French Fries	$ .68	Coke	$ .50
With Cheese	1.10			Lg. Coke	.60
Lettuce and		Baked Beans	.82		
Tomato Extra	.20			Orange	.50
Triple Delight	2.53	Cottage Cheese	.57	Lemon	.50
With Cheese	2.70	Tossed Salad	.65		
Cheese Plate — for				Coffee	.40
Children under 12.		Chili	.91	Milk	.45
Cheese sandwich and					
french fries	1.29	Chili with Cheese	1.11	Shake	.65

DESSERTS		SPECIAL			
Brownie	.53	Burger Delight Platter		Burger	
Cheesecake	.95	— Comes with Burger,		Hut	
Strawberry, Vanilla,		French Fries and		For The	
Chocolate, Butterrum		Baked Beans	2.27	Finest	
Sundae	.88			Foods	

Using the prices given on the Burger Hut menu, answer these questions.

1. Alice wants to order a supper of a burger delight, french fries and baked beans. Will it cost her more or less to order the burger delight platter or to order the items separately?

    ○   more   ○   less

    How much will the bill total if she orders the 3 items separately?

    ○ $2.87   ○ $2.47   ○ $2.77

2. How much change from a $5.00 bill will Alice receive if she orders the burger delight platter?
    _____

3. With the change she receives, she also orders a small orange drink and a strawberry sundae. How much money does she have left? _____

4. A father and his 10 year old son go to the Burger Hut after a football game. The father wants a triple delight with cheese, lettuce and tomato, a regular coke and a brownie. The son wants a cheese plate and a chocolate shake. How much will their lunch cost? _____

5. What would you like for lunch today? You may only spend $3.00. List the items you would order and total the bill.

Item	Price
_____	_____
_____	_____
_____	_____
Total	_____
Change	_____

Spending Money

SHIRTS SALE

Sizes S,M,L,XL
Buy 1 PRICE $18.99
Buy more than one PRICE $16.99
SAVE!

JOHNSON'S FINEST

NAME AND ADDRESS—PLEASE PRINT CLEARLY

Name

Complete Address

Phone Number   Charge Number

List each item separately. Store will figure sales tax on charges.

How Many	Name of Item	Color	Size	Price
			Total	

BLACK·BROWN·BLUE
MEN'S BELTS NOW $8.00 was $10.00
SIZES 28, 30, 32, 34, 36

Leather Handbags
Through November 10 only $7.99
after that date $10.99
Tan   Burgundy

Using the following information, please fill in the order form and work the problems.

On October 10, Jane Roberts decides to send in an order to a catalog store, planning to buy presents for several people in her family. She fills out the order form and sends it in the mail.

Jane Roberts, 727 West Pine Road, Apt. 6, Newville, Mass. 46422, phone 737-220-0040, store charge number 2 73312 46551 7. Jane orders: 1 burgundy handbag for herself, 1 tan handbag for her sister Alice, 1 navy shirt (size M) for her brother Ted and 2 matching green shirts (size S) for her twin brothers Andy and Alan.

1. If Jane buys a handbag after November 10, how much more will it cost? _____

2. How much would 3 handbags cost before November 10? _____
   After November 10? _____

3. Jane wants to buy a belt for her father. What is the catalog price when she orders?
   _____ What would the belt have cost her before it went on sale? _____

4. 1 shirt costs _____. How much would 3 shirts cost? _____

5. Can Jane buy 1 shirt and 1 belt for less than $30.00? _____
   What will the total price be? _____
   How much change should she receive from her $30.00? _____

6. Which would cost more, 1 belt and 1 shirt, or 2 belts. _____
   How much more? _____

7. Does Jane need to figure tax on this order if she charges it? _____

Reading A Schedule

Jane Quinn	M	TU	W	TH	F
8:10 8:40	English	English	Study Hall	English	English
8:45 9:15	Science	Home Ec.	Science	Home Ec.	Science
9:20 9:50	Science	Study Hall	Science	Study Hall	Science
9:55 10:25	Math	Math	Math	Math	Math
10:30 11:00	History	History	Study Hall	History	Health
11:05 11:40	Art	Art	Study Hall	Art	Study Hall
11:45 12:00	Break	Break	Break	Break	Break

1. Jane is adding up the times she spends in each class each week. How much time does she spend in:

   English _____   Math _____   Art _____   Home Ec. _____

   Science _____   History _____   Health _____

2. Does Jane spend more than 2 hours a week in study hall? _____

   How much more? _____

3. How much time is allowed to go from one class to the next? _____

4. On Tuesday, does Jane spend time in science? _____ In health? _____

   In history? _____

5. Are all of Jane's periods the same length? _____

6. English classes meet:

   ○ every day   ○ four days out of five   ○ three days

7. Jane has science:

   ○ 60 minutes daily   ○ 30 minutes daily   ○ 60 minutes three days a week

8. This schedule shows that Jane is in school:

   ○ 4 hours a day   ○ 3 hours, 50 minutes a day   ○ 35 hours a week

9. Jane has math a total of:

   ○ 40 minutes a day   ○ $2\frac{1}{2}$ hours a week   ○ 60 minutes a day

10. The ratio of math periods to history periods per week is:

    ○ 5 to 4   ○ 3 to 5   ○ 5 to 3

11. What is the ratio of hours spent in math to English?

    ○ 30 minutes to 30   ○ $2\frac{1}{2}$ hours to 2 hours   ○ 4 hours to 5 hours

              Competency Skills—Math

Studying Graphs

Jim receives an allowance of $8.00 each week. He has divided it into 6 parts to help himself spend it wisely.

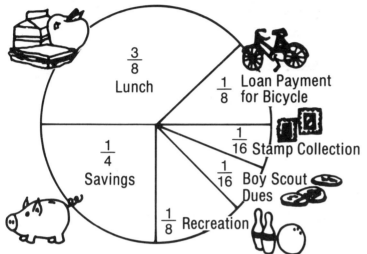

Answer the following questions using the graph above.

1. On what item does Jim spend the most money each week? _____
   How much does he spend on this? _____
   On what 2 items does he spend the least money? _____
   What it the total amount he spends on these? _____

2. Does the total amount spent on loan repayment and recreation equal the amount for savings? _____
   How much more or less? _____

3. What dollar amount does $\frac{1}{4}$ of $8.00 represent? _____
   $\frac{1}{8}$ of $8.00? _____
   $\frac{1}{16}$ of $8.00? _____

4. When Jim has paid his Boy Scout dues and his lunch money for the week, how much does he have left? _____

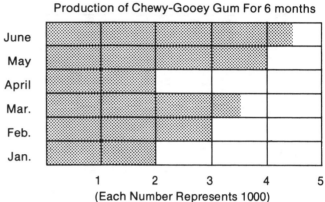

Production of Chewy-Gooey Gum For 6 months

(Each Number Represents 1000)

1. In January, Mr. Miles opened a Chewy-Gooey Gum Factory. Because it was the first month of operation, the total number of packs produced was a small amount. How many packs were produced in January? _____

2. In February the production rate increased. How many more packs were produced this month? _____

3. Mr. Miles was pleased to discover that March was an even better month than the previous two. How many packs were produced in March? _____

4. The results for April were the same as for _____ .

5. What was the total amount manufactured in January and February? _____
   Was it greater or less than the amount manufactured in June? _____

Sports Math

BASEBALL		
TEAM	WON	LOST
BREWERS	85	15
METS	78	22
YANKEES	70	30
WHITE SOX	65	35
DODGERS	62	38

FOOTBALL		
TEAM	WON	LOST
COWBOYS	10	4
CHARGERS	8	6
CARDINALS	7	7
COLTS	6	8
LIONS	4	10
VIKINGS	3	11

When figuring a team's percentage, add the total number of games played. Divide the number of games won by the total number of games played. Round the answer to three decimal places.

For example: Won — 63 games
Lost — 27 games
90 games played

.700
90) 63.00

Use the above charts to figure these team percentages. Fill in the circle in front of the correct answer.

1. The Cowboys team percentage is:
   ○ .714   ○ .814   ○ .700

2. The Cardinals team percentage is:
   ○ .250   ○ .100   ○ .500

3. If a team has won and lost an equal number of games, the percentage will be:
   ○ .1000   ○ .500   ○ .100

4. The Colts have a team percentage of:
   ○ .420   ○ .429   ○ .350

5. Figure these team percentages.
   Won — 28   Won —110   Won — 32
   Lost — 42   Lost — 23   Lost — 18
   Total games — _____   Total games — _____   Total games — _____
   Percentage — _____   Percentage — _____   Percentage — _____

In the game of bowling, team averages, rather than percentages, determine placement. For example, if Richard's team members bowled games of 170, 128, 166, and 182, the team total is 646. To find the team average, divide 646 by 4. Richard's team has an average of 161.5.

Figure the averages for these bowling teams. Be sure to round decimals to the tenths place.

1. Ken's team has six bowlers. Their scores are 196, 177, 145, 201, 152, and 116. The team average is:
   ○ 166   ○ 164.5   ○ 165.4

2. Marion's team of three members bowled 112, 131, and 98. The team average is:
   ○ 113.7   ○ 113   ○ 112.6

3. The Cub Scouts bowled 92, 88, 74, 62, 59, 81, 92, and 77. The team average is:
   ○ 50   ○ 52.4   ○ 78.1

Computing Sales Tax

States have different tax rates. This rate is a percentage charged to the customer for each dollar spent. A 6% sales tax means that 6% or .06 on each dollar spent is charged additionally for taxes.

For example:

$1.00	$4.00	$9.50	$5.75
× .06	× .06	× .06	× .06
.0600 or 6¢	☐	☐	☐

This amount is then added to the sale price. An article selling for a dollar would cost $1.06 and an article selling for $2.00 would cost $2.12.

Using a 6% sales tax, solve these problems.

1. Purchases: $5.75
                      3.25
                 + .82   ☐ Subtotal

   Subtotal ☐   ☐ × .06

   ☐ + ☐ = ☐ Final Cost

2. Purchases: $ .75
                       1.23
                 + 4.08   ☐ Subtotal

   Subtotal ☐   ☐ × .06

   ☐ + ☐ = ☐ Final Cost

3. Complete the chart.

Article	Unit Price	Quantity	Cost
Pencils	$.12	4	
Erasers	$.08	6	
Blotters		2	$.50
Glue		2	$1.72
		Total	

4. How much sales tax at 6% would be paid on the total for all the articles in #3?

   _____

Change these sales tax percentages to decimals:

1. 2% = _____   3. 7% = _____
2. 4% = _____   4. 5% = _____

1. What is 2% of $2.00?   ○ $.02   ○ $.04   ○ $.08
2. What is 7% of $7.00?   ○ $.07   ○ $.14   ○ $.49
3. What is the sales tax on $8.00 if the tax rate is 4% ?
                           ○ $.12   ○ $.32   ○ $.04
4. What is 5% of $10.00?   ○ $.05   ○ $.50   ○ $.20
5. What is the difference in the tax that is paid on a $5.00 purchase at 4% sales tax and a $5.00 purchase at a 2% sales tax?
                           ○ $.10   ○ $.02   ○ $.20

Complete this chart.

Price	Rate of Tax	Sales tax	Total Cost
$12.00	4%		
$3.00	5%		
$8.00	6%		

                                       Competency Skills—Math

Consumer Discounts

To figure the amount of discount, multiply the percentage, or rate of discount, by the selling price. Then subtract the amount reduced from the original price. The answer is the new price.

For example:
```
  $85.00   (coat)                    $85.00   (original price)
   x .50   (discount rate)          -42.50   (amount reduced)
    0000                             $42.50   (new price for the coat)
   42500
 $42.5000  (amount reduced)
```

Using the illustration above, answer the following questions.

1. At an end of summer sale, Maggie decided to buy a bathing suit which was originally priced at $26.00, a pair of tennis shoes which had been $17.00, and a scarf, marked down from $10.00. Figure the price on each item and then the total bill.

article	bathing suit	shoes	scarf
original price			
discount rate (%)			
amount reduced			
new price			

The total bill for the three items would be_____ .

2. What will the savings be on a winter coat which originally sold for $125.00? _____

3. Judy wants to buy 5 scarves to give as Christmas presents. If each scarf originally cost $2.00, what will she have to pay for one scarf? _____ For all five scarves?_____

4. 10% off a $3.00 item is equal to   ○ 10¢   ○ 30¢   ○ 40¢

    15% off a $3.00 item is equal to   ○ 45¢   ○ 18¢   ○ $1.00

    Does Matt save more money with a 10% discount or a 15% discount?_____

5. The Eagle Sports Shop is selling all of its stock at a 10% discount. After every day of the sale the remaining items are each marked down an additional 10% for each day they are not sold. If a football sold for $19.00 before the sale, what will it sell for the first day of the sale? _____ What will be the new price the second day? _____

Travel Trivia

Scale: $\frac{1}{2}'' = 1$ mile

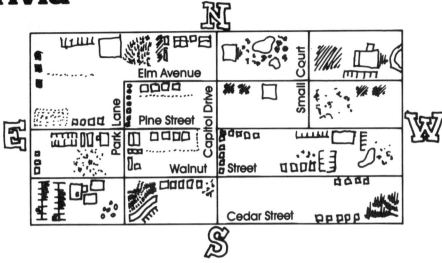

Using the map above, answer the following questions.

1. How long is Elm Avenue on this map? _____
2. Cedar Street is how many miles longer than Elm Avenue? _____
3. Small Court is _____ inch(es) long and _____ miles on this map.
4. Which streets run in an east/west direction? _____
5. How many miles would a street that measures $1\frac{1}{2}$ inches be on this map? _____
6. If John traveled from the corner of Park Lane and Cedar Street to the intersection of Elm Avenue and Small Court, how many miles would he travel? _____
7. If a road sign said "Highway 70 - 12 miles ahead", how many inches would represent 12 miles if the map scale is $\frac{1}{2}$ inch represents one mile? _____

These cars each receive an average MPG or miles per gallon. This is the distance a car can travel on one gallon of gas. For example, 22 MPG means the car will travel 22 miles on a gallon of gas. The other number given is the number of gallons the car's gas tank will hold. Use the figures given below to fill out the chart.

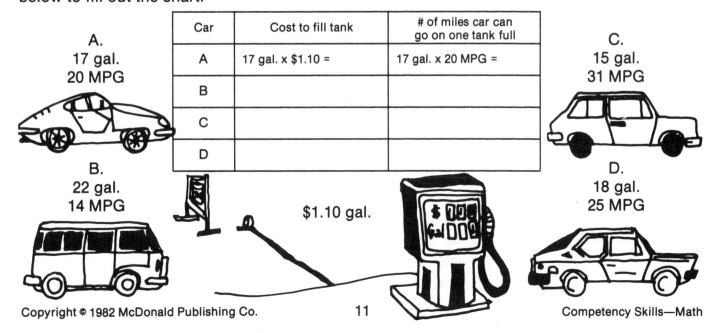

A.
17 gal.
20 MPG

B.
22 gal.
14 MPG

C.
15 gal.
31 MPG

D.
18 gal.
25 MPG

$1.10 gal.

Car	Cost to fill tank	# of miles car can go on one tank full
A	17 gal. x $1.10 =	17 gal. x 20 MPG =
B		
C		
D		

Review Test

Choose the correct answer for each question.

1. If the sales tax is 5%, how much tax would Joan pay on a $13.00 purchase?
   - ○ 35¢
   - ○ 65¢
   - ○ 15¢
   - ○ no answer given

2. Mildred bought a bathing suit for $29.45. How much change would she receive from a $50.00 bill?
   - ○ $30.55
   - ○ $21.55
   - ○ $20.55
   - ○ no answer given

3. Compute the 6% sales tax on items costing $5.25 and $1.25.
   - ○ 45¢
   - ○ 35¢
   - ○ 39¢
   - ○ 31¢

4. Deposit $114.89, $17.45, and $14.72 into a checking account. The total deposit is:
   - ○ $147.06
   - ○ $140.76
   - ○ $146.07
   - ○ $145.00

5. Jane has a reading class from 9:35 until 11:05. How long is her class?
   - ○ one hour ten minutes
   - ○ one hour thirty minutes
   - ○ one hour thirty-five minutes
   - ○ one hour five minutes

6. Subtract checks of $23.00, $117.17, and $8.03 from a checking account balance of $500.00.
   - ○ $350.01
   - ○ $35.81
   - ○ $351.80
   - ○ $404.22

7. $\frac{1}{4}$ cup flour and $\frac{1}{2}$ cup sugar equals how many cups of dry ingredients?
   - ○ 1 cup
   - ○ $1\frac{1}{2}$ cups
   - ○ $\frac{2}{3}$ cup
   - ○ $\frac{3}{4}$ cup

8. On a map using a scale of 1 inch representing 150 miles, how many inches equals 600 miles?
   - ○ 2 inches
   - ○ 6 inches
   - ○ 4 inches
   - ○ no answer given

9. If a team has won 115 games and lost 88 games, what is the team percentage? (Round to the nearest hundredth.)
   - ○ .203
   - ○ .567
   - ○ .333
   - ○ .714

10. Which of these percentages would be the highest?
    - ○ .565
    - ○ .702
    - ○ .656
    - ○ .556

11. Average these bowling scores: 194, 213, 177, and 203.
    - ○ 196.8
    - ○ 200
    - ○ 196

12. Which is a better buy, a notebook costing $1.98 and selling at a 10% discount or a $2.00 notebook selling at a 15% discount?
    - ○ the $1.98 notebook
    - ○ the $2.00 notebook
    - ○ they are the same

13. If Irene doubles the amount of a recipe that calls for two-thirds cup of sugar, how much sugar will she need?
    - ○ 1 cup
    - ○ $1\frac{1}{4}$ cups
    - ○ $1\frac{1}{3}$ cups
    - ○ $1\frac{2}{3}$ cups

14. If a car has a 22 gallon gas tank and gasoline is $1.15 a gallon, how much will it cost to fill the tank?
    - ○ $26.00
    - ○ $25.30
    - ○ $30.00
    - ○ $33.00

15. How far could the car in #14 travel on a tank of gas if it gets 12 miles to the gallon?
    - ○ 300 miles
    - ○ 244 miles
    - ○ 284 miles
    - ○ 264 miles

16. John started raking leaves at 10:30 in the morning. He finished at 2:00 in the afternoon. How long did he work?
    - ○ 4 hours
    - ○ 4 hours 15 minutes
    - ○ 5 hours
    - ○ 3 hours 30 minutes

Name _____

Using Fractions

Many products have instructions for preparation on the back of the package. Often these instructions tell how to prepare a number of servings, but occasionally you may have to figure out amounts needed for larger or smaller numbers of servings.

Fill in this chart and then answer the questions.

Item	2 Servings	4 Servings	6 Servings
Water	$\frac{2}{3}$ cup		
Milk	$\frac{1}{3}$ cup	$\frac{2}{3}$ cup	
Butter	1 Tbsp.		3 Tbsp.
Salt	$\frac{1}{4}$ tsp.	$\frac{1}{2}$ tsp.	
Potato Flakes	1 cup		

1. Bill needs to fix mashed potatoes for the dinner he is preparing. If there are four people in the family, how will he fill in this chart? Some of the answers have been done for him.

2. How many cups of potato flakes would be needed to make 12 servings? _____

3. How much more water is used than milk? _____

4. What is the total number of cups of ingredients used when making four servings? _____

5. How much water would be used if the recipe was tripled? _____

   quadrupled? _____

6. Reduce these fractions to lowest terms.

   $\frac{3}{9}$ = $\frac{10}{12}$ = $\frac{8}{10}$ = $\frac{75}{100}$ = $\frac{15}{20}$ = $\frac{9}{27}$ =

   $\frac{45}{50}$ = $\frac{11}{22}$ = $\frac{33}{99}$ = $\frac{4}{28}$ = $\frac{5}{25}$ = $\frac{3}{18}$ =

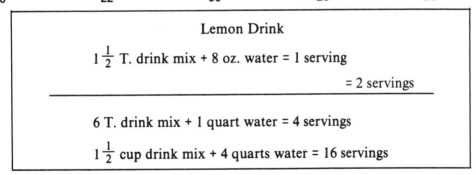

Lemon Drink
$1\frac{1}{2}$ T. drink mix + 8 oz. water = 1 serving
= 2 servings
6 T. drink mix + 1 quart water = 4 servings
$1\frac{1}{2}$ cup drink mix + 4 quarts water = 16 servings

1. Janet and Molly are thirsty for some lemon drink. The chart on the drink mix does not tell them how to make lemon drink for 2 servings. How much drink mix and water will they need? Fill in the chart.

2. $1\frac{1}{2}$ T. multiplied by 3 equals: ○ 4 T.   ○ 5 T.   ○ $4\frac{1}{2}$ T.

3. $1\frac{1}{2}$ T. multiplied by 4 equals: ○ 6 T.   ○ $5\frac{1}{2}$ T.   ○ $6\frac{1}{2}$ T.

4. What is $1\frac{2}{3}$ divided by 2?   ○ $\frac{5}{6}$ ○ $\frac{2}{3}$ ○ $\frac{3}{4}$

Geometric Figures

Identify these figures. Fill in the circle in front of the correct answer.

1.
This is a
- ○ square.
- ○ rectangle.
- ○ trapezoid.

2.
This is a
- ○ circle.
- ○ cone.
- ○ cylinder.

3.
This is a
- ○ cube.
- ○ square.
- ○ pentagon.

4.
This is a
- ○ trapezoid.
- ○ rectangle.
- ○ parallelogram.

5.
These lines are
- ○ perpendicular.
- ○ parallel.
- ○ intersecting.

6.
This angle is
- ○ 75°.
- ○ 100°.
- ○ 90°.

7.
A triangle has
- ○ 180°.
- ○ 100°.
- ○ 300°.

8.
This triangle has
- ○ a 90° angle.
- ○ three equal angles.
- ○ two equal angles.

9.
This is a
- ○ ray.
- ○ angle.
- ○ line segment.

10.
This is a
- ○ pentagon.
- ○ hexagon.
- ○ octagon.

11.
If a triangle has one 60° angle, then
- ○ it has a 90° angle and a 20° angle.
- ○ it has 2 more 60° angles.
- ○ it has two 45° angles.

12.
This figure has
- ○ 180°.
- ○ 200°.
- ○ 360°.

13.
This figure has
- ○ 360°.
- ○ 100°.
- ○ 90°.

14. A hexagon has
- ○ 4 sides.
- ○ 5 sides.
- ○ 6 sides.

15. An octagon has
- ○ 6 sides.
- ○ 8 sides.
- ○ 9 sides.

16. A quadrilateral has
- ○ 2 sides.
- ○ 4 sides.
- ○ many sides.

17. A parallelogram has
- ○ 4 right angles.
- ○ opposite sides parallel.
- ○ 6 sides.

18. Perpendicular lines
- ○ form right angles.
- ○ are the same length.
- ○ never meet.

19. A diameter of a circle
- ○ passes through the center of a circle.
- ○ goes all around the circle.
- ○ begins in the center of a circle.

20. The circumference of a circle measures
- ○ the area inside the circle.
- ○ the distance around the circle.
- ○ half of the circle.

Name _____

Perimeter, Area, and Volume

Figure A

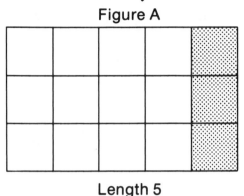

Width 3

Length 5

Figure B

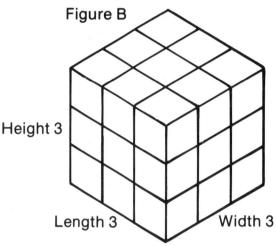

Height 3

Length 3   Width 3

Area = length × width
Perimeter = 2 lengths + 2 widths
Volume = length × width × height

Using the information that is given above, answer the following questions.

1. What is the area of figure A.

   ○ 15 square units   ○ 18 square units   ○ 8 square units

2. If figure A were the drawing of a floor, how many floor tiles would George have to buy to cover the floor? Each tile is equal to one square unit. _____

3. What is the perimeter of figure A?

   ○ 15 units   ○ 16 units   ○ 8 units

4. What is the area of the shaded part of figure A? _____

5. In figure B, what is the volume or number of cubic units? _____

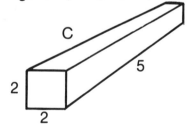 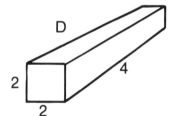 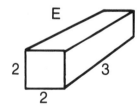

6. Match the volume with the letter.   C   16 cubic units
                                           D   12 cubic units
                                           E   20 cubic units

7.

A terrace measures 4′ by 11′. If the owner wants to double the size of the terrace, how large would it be? _____
If he wants to make it $\frac{1}{2}$ the original size, how large will it be?

_____

8. What amount of fencing will completely surround the terrace shown above and leave extra material?   ○ 28′   ○ 15′   ○ 32′

   How much fencing will be left over? _____

Name _____

Best Buys

Products are available in various sizes at different prices per unit. The smart shopper figures out which size represents the best buy.

To decide which is the best buy, find the cost for one ounce (or pound or unit) and then compare.

For example:

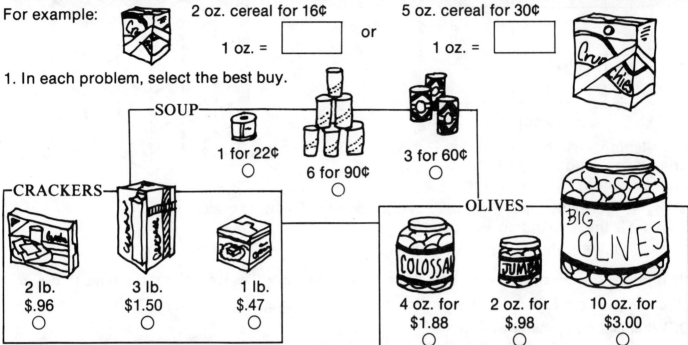

2 oz. cereal for 16¢

1 oz. = [ ] or 5 oz. cereal for 30¢

1 oz. = [ ]

1. In each problem, select the best buy.

SOUP

1 for 22¢ ○

6 for 90¢ ○

3 for 60¢ ○

CRACKERS

2 lb.	3 lb.	1 lb.
$.96	$1.50	$.47
○	○	○

OLIVES

4 oz. for	2 oz. for	10 oz. for
$1.88	$.98	$3.00
○	○	○

2. If Ann selects the best buy in each of the 3 selections shown above, what will her total bill be?

_____

In figuring the cost of one item, the smart shopper knows that the extra penny goes to the store. For example, if applesauce sells at 2 jars for 49¢, one jar costs 25¢, not 24¢.
Using this information, fill in the chart below.

Item	Amount	Total Cost	Cost per Unit, Ounce or Pound
orange juice	2 cans for	$.79	
towels	3 rolls		$.40
toothpaste		$2.50	$1.25
dog food	25 lb. bag	$8.00	
pizza sauce		$2.58	$1.29
pizza crust	2 boxes		$.77
pepperoni	1 lb.	$3.00	
soda	6 cans		$.17
chips	2 for price of one special		$1.00
lettuce	2 heads for	$.67	

Earnings and Deductions

Attached to every paycheck is a stub which gives information about the amount the employee earned, the amount deducted from the check, and the actual amount taken home. Paychecks may be issued weekly, every two weeks, or monthly. The information on a paycheck is itemized for every pay period and for the year-to-date (the total thus far in the year). These definitions will help you understand the deductions and other categories on a paycheck stub.

RATE: The rate is the amount paid for each hour, day, or month. For example, Jane babysits at the rate of $1.50 an hour. Ted is paid at the rate of $55.00 per week.

HOURS: The hours indicate the number of hours the employee worked if he was paid by the hour.

EARNINGS: The earnings are the amount of money earned during the pay period.

GROSS PAY: The gross pay is the amount earned before deductions.

NET PAY: The net pay is the amount the employee ends up with after deductions.

STATE WITHHOLDING: The state withholding tax is about 5% of the total earnings. The state uses this money to finance state programs.

FICA: The FICA tax is about a 6% tax that is used for Social Security.

FEDERAL WITHHOLDING: The federal withholding tax is the largest deduction. This is a United States government tax of about 20% and it is used to support government programs.

Study this paycheck stub and answer the questions. You will need to use the terms and definitions above.

RATE	HOURS	EARNINGS	NAME: Jennifer Smithers		DATE: 6/30/85
$120.00		$120.00	State Withholding	FICA	Federal Withholding
			$6.00	$7.20	$24.00
Gross Pay		Net Pay	Gross Pay	State Withholding / FICA	Federal Withholding
$120.00		$82.80	$720.00	$36.00 / $43.20	$144.00

◄————————YEAR TO DATE————————►

Year-to-date columns (left to right): Gross Pay $720.00, State Withholding $36.00, FICA $43.20, Federal Withholding $144.00.

1. Are the earnings and the gross pay equal? _____

2. What is the largest amount deducted from a paycheck? _____

3. Net pay means: _____

4. Which is the larger deduction, the FICA tax or the state withholding tax? _____

5. On the stub above, what was the total amount of deductions for the pay period?

_____

6. What is the year-to-date information on a paycheck stub? _____

_____

7. 5% of $120.00 is: ○ $7.20   ○ $24.00   ○ $6.00

8. How many months has Jennifer been working?   ○ 4   ○ 8   ○ 6

Name _____   **Using Temperature and Percentage**

Studying Charts

Weather reports are part of our everyday life. In order to understand them fully we need to know how to use percentages, interpret charts, and read thermometers, both Celsius and Fahrenheit. *Study the weather report, the rainfall chart, and the temperature chart and then answer the questions.*

"The weather will be cloudy. There is a 40% chance of rain Friday, a 60% chance of rain Friday night, and a 20% chance of rain early Saturday morning. The temperature will be 75° on Friday afternoon, 50° Friday night, and 60° early Saturday morning."

Normal Rainfall for 5 Months

INCHES OF RAINFALL: 0 1 2 3 4 5

MAY   JUNE   JULY   AUGUST   SEPT.

	CELSIUS	FAHRENHEIT
BOILING POINT	100° C	212° F
FREEZING POINT	0° C	32° F
HUMAN TEMPERATURE	37° C	98.6° F

1. If a class picnic is planned for Friday or Saturday, depending on the weather, which would be the better day to have it? _____

2. If the weatherman was certain it would rain, what percent would he give?
   ○ the total of 40%, 20%, and 60%   ○ 50%   ○ 100%

3. According to the rainfall chart, which is the wettest month?_____
   How many inches did it rain that month? _____

4. What is the total rainfall for May, July, August, and September?_____

5. Is a 50% chance of rain a higher chance than a 35% chance?_____

6. Which months had equal rainfalls? _____

7. According to the weather report, how much warmer would it be on Friday afternoon than on Friday night? _____

8. How many degrees are there between the freezing point and the boiling point on a Celsius thermometer? _____ On a Fahrenheit thermometer? _____

9. If the weatherman says that the temperature is 59 degrees Fahrenheit, will the temperature in Celsius degrees be a number larger or smaller than 59? _____

10. If George had a temperature of 104° Fahrenheit, how many degrees is that above the normal temperature for a human being? _____

Copyright © 1982 McDonald Publishing Co.   18   Competency Skills—Math

Working With Decimals

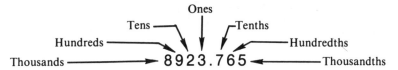

Use the above example to answer the questions. Fill in the circle in front of the correct answer.

1. What number is in the hundreds place?
   - ○ 8   ○ 9
   - ○ 7   ○ 6

2. What number is in the thousandths place?
   - ○ 8   ○ 6
   - ○ 5   ○ 7

3. What would this number be if .01 was added to it?
   - ○ 8924.765   ○ 8923.766
   - ○ 8923.775   ○ 8923.865

4. What would the new number be if 1000 was added to it?
   - ○ 9923.765   ○ 8933.765
   - ○ 8923.865   ○ 9923.665

5. Round this number to the nearest tenth.
   - ○ 8923.7   ○ 8923.8
   - ○ 8923.6   ○ 8923.86

Write the correct decimal for each sum. For example: $4 + \frac{2}{10} = 4.2$

1. $5 + \frac{2}{10} =$ 4. $605 + \frac{0}{10} + \frac{3}{100} =$
2. $18 + \frac{3}{10} + \frac{5}{100} =$ 5. $1525 + \frac{5}{10} =$
3. $235 + \frac{0}{10} + \frac{8}{100} =$ 6. $200 + \frac{4}{10} + \frac{8}{100} + \frac{9}{1000} =$

Write these decimals as mixed numbers. For example: $25.25 = 25\frac{25}{100}$

1. 125.009 =   4. 5.5 =
2. 76.7 =   5. 999.9 =
3. 900.1 =   6. 1.2 =

Write these fractions as percents.

1. $\frac{3}{4} =$ 3. $\frac{1}{2} =$ 5. $\frac{3}{5} =$ 7. $\frac{1}{4} =$
2. $\frac{1}{8} =$ 4. $\frac{9}{10} =$ 6. $\frac{2}{3} =$ 8. $\frac{1}{3} =$

Add these numbers.

1. 45.15 + 2.3 + 161.9 =   4. 7.2 + 6.8 + 2.11 =
2. 34.44 + 1.001 =   5. 55.05 + 2.04 =
3. 687.005 + 234.115 =   6. 79.64 + .23 =

Compute these multiplication problems.

1. 57.2 × 3 =   3. 90.00 × .04 =
2. 77.04 × 3.5 =   4. .05 × .08 =

        19   Competency Skills—Math

Review Test
Fill in the circle in front of the correct answer.

1. Add these fractions: $\frac{9}{10} + \frac{3}{5} =$ ○ $1\frac{2}{5}$ ○ $1\frac{1}{2}$ ○ $1\frac{3}{10}$

2. Subtract 120.35 from 552.89.
   ○ 673.24   ○ 432.54   ○ 603.45   ○ no answer given

3. $4\frac{1}{4} - \frac{1}{2} =$ ○ 4   ○ $3\frac{1}{2}$ ○ $3\frac{1}{4}$ ○ $3\frac{3}{4}$

4. What is the perimeter of a room 23' x 19'?
   ○ 573 feet   ○ 373 feet   ○ 460 feet   ○ 437 feet

5. Perpendicular lines are lines that:
   ○ cross each other   ○ are equal distance from each other
   ○ intersect at right angles ○ have equal length

6. Find the volume of a cube with a length of 12", a width of 12", and a height of 12".
   ○ 1444 sq. in.   ○ 1206 sq. in.   ○ 1728 sq. in.   ○ 1800 sq. in.

7. If bird seed is on sale in 25 lb. bags selling for $6.50 and 5 lb. bags selling for 25¢ a lb., which is the better buy?
   ○ 25 lb. bag   ○ 5 lb. bag

8. In problem #7, how much does the buyer save if he purchases the better buy?
   ○ 2¢ a lb.   ○ 1¢ a lb.   ○ 5¢ a lb.   ○ 3¢ a lb.

9. If Louise babysits a total of 15 hours over the weekend and she charges $1.25 an hour, how much does she earn?
   ○ $20.00   ○ $17.75   ○ $18.75   ○ $21.75

10. If the temperature on Monday was 65°, Tuesday was 57°, Wednesday was 63°, then the average temperature for these three days was:
    ○ 60°   ○ 55°   ○ 57.7°   ○ 61.7°

11. Find the perimeter of a room that has a length of 24.5 feet and a width of 13 feet.
    ○ 218 feet   ○ 75 feet   ○ 183 feet   ○ 180 feet

12. Multiply these fractions: $\frac{3}{4} \times \frac{5}{6} =$
    ○ $\frac{5}{6}$ ○ $\frac{8}{10}$ ○ $\frac{15}{10}$ ○ $\frac{5}{8}$

13. .25 written as a fraction is:
    ○ $\frac{2}{3}$ ○ $\frac{3}{4}$ ○ $\frac{1}{4}$ ○ $\frac{5}{6}$

14. If an article selling for $112.00 is marked 50% off, the new price is:
    ○ $65.00   ○ $54.00   ○ $56.00   ○ $50.50

15. Compute: $\frac{11}{20} \div \frac{1}{2} =$ ○ $1\frac{1}{10}$ ○ $1\frac{1}{5}$ ○ $1\frac{2}{11}$ ○ $1\frac{22}{23}$

16. Team A has won 45 games and lost 5. Team B has won 40 games and lost 10. Which of the following statements is true?
    ○ Team A has played more games.   ○ Team A lost the most games.
    ○ Team A has won a higher   ○ Team A and Team B have equal
       percentage of games.   percentages.